STRANGE HILL HIGH

FREE MITCHELL MASK

W0008059

YOU WILL NEED:

- THIN ELASTIC, WOOL OR STRING
- SCISSORS
- STICKY TAPE

INSTRUCTIONS:

1. PULL OUT THE MASK PAGE OPPOSITE.
2. POP OUT THE MASK.
3. CUT ENOUGH ELASTIC / WOOL / STRING TO FIT AROUND THE BACK OF YOUR HEAD.
4. ATTACH TO THE BACK OF THE MASK WITH SOME STICKY TAPE.
5. HAVE FUN WITH YOUR NEW MASK!

SCISSORS ARE SHARP! ASK AN ADULT FOR HELP BEFORE USING.

CONTENTS

Published 2014. Pedigree Books Limited, Beech Hill House, Walnut Gardens, Exeter, Devon EX4 4DH. www.pedigreebooks.com – books@pedigreegroup.co.uk
The Pedigree trademark, email and website addresses, are the sole and exclusive properties of Pedigree Group Limited, used under licence in this publication.
STRANGE HILL HIGH word and device marks are trade marks of the British Broadcasting Corporation. © 2014 BBC. Licensed by FremantleMedia Limited.
The "BBC" word mark and logo are trade marks of the British Broadcasting Corporation and are used under licence. BBC Logo © BBC 1996.

FREMANTLEMEDIA BBC

HOW MANY OF THESE WEIRD CHARACTERS CAN YOU FIND THROUGHOUT THIS BOOK? SPOTTING RANDOM THINGS IS A SPORT AT STRANGE HILL HIGH!

PG........

THE EMBARRASSMENT

PG........

CHRISTMAS ELF LEADER

PG........

KEN KONG

PG........

MITCHELL JUNIOR

PG........

JERKEY

Pedigree®

WELCOME TO THE WEIRDNESS

Hello, stranger. The sneaky students and freaky faculty at Strange Hill High invite you to explore their peculiar school. There is no easy way to explain it; you've got to see it with your own googly eyes.

You are weirdly welcome to enter the creepy corridors of the wackiest school in the world, but enter at your own risk.... Things occasionally go missing, explode or hover in mid-air. Here odd is ordinary and time can't be trusted. Whirlpools of weirdness suck you in and unnatural adventures lurk round the bend. So smash the system, embrace the strangeness and geek up on crazy! Hurrah for hilarity!

MEH! CHILL OUT COMRADES. STICK WITH CAPTAIN MITCHELL! I'VE FIGURED OUT HOW TO SURVIVE THIS SCHOOL.

YOU'LL NEVER FIND LIFE STRANGER THAN AT STRANGE HILL HIGH.
KEEP THE LIGHTS ON... SOMETHING LOOPY IS COMING THIS WAY...
N.I.M.R.O.D. Compact

YO, MITCHELL!

Mitchell is a homework-dodging, monster-fighting **COOL DUDE.** At SHH, things are often super scary and stink of strange, but Mitchell takes it all with a bounce in his trainer-wearing stride.

He randomly walks into disaster on a regular basis, so Mitchell's becoming a master at tackling mayhem with his trademark offbeat banter. Oh, he's good at yo-yo flicks and busting sweet tricks on his skateboard too. Mitchell doesn't mind a little **TANTALISING TERROR** to keep him on his toes – madness is better than normal.

Some students say his approach to study is mellow (Mitchell's favourite subject is lunch), although his best mate Becky doesn't mind calling him plain lazy to his face. Mitchell is clever in an alternative way – it's amazing how fast his brain works to avoid work.

Tyson: I got a problem. I got a woodwork deadline and I ain't got no woodwork. So I got thinking, who'd have some woodwork?
Mitchell: Errr, Woody?
Tyson: Who's Woody?
Mitchell: Woody the woodwork worker.
Tyson: Would Woody have some woodwork?
Mitchell: I don't know, would he?
Tyson: Are you mocking me?
Mitchell: Yeah.

action
beats
study

Not to care is a talent you're born with and I don't care enough to pass it on.

**WHASSUP?
SOMEBODY
EXPLODE?**

No need to get all logical with me!

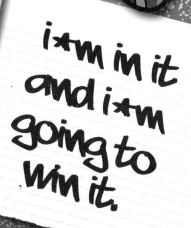

i*m in it and i*m going to win it.

**I GET BORED
WITH ALL THIS
THINKY TALK**

**STAND BY FOR
TANNER TIME!**

You can let ignorance stand in your way, or you can use it to your advantage.

squeaking by is my speciality

i*m not late, i*m alternatively early

**NEMO TO SPIDERMAN. CLIMBING UP THE INSIDE OF A STRUCTURE
IS A LOT EASIER THAN CLIMBING UP THE OUTSIDE.**

IT'S BECKY!

Becky Butters is the greatest pinky-haired friend anyone could have. Becky's an expert at navigating the horrors in the halls and knows all about the jungle-like antics at the bizarre school, although new levels of **BONKERS** continue to surprise her.

Every day Mitchell astonishes her by his ability to forget work! So Becky is prepared for anything and will always watch his back, adding her enthusiasm and quick wit to Mitchell's heroics.

When she isn't dodging dripping goo or solving secret mysteries with **GRADE A BECKY-NESS**, Becky makes sure she completes her school projects on time. Determined to stay on track to become school president, university president and then prime minister, Becky is bursting with ideas to save the planet!

Becky: You don't scare me! You're just my anxieties and fears rolled up into one ugly monster!
Grackle: Take that back!
Becky: And if I ignore you, you'll go away!
Grackle: Look at me!
Becky: No, I'm ignoring you. La la la la la.
Grackle: No! Not ignoring and horrible singing! Noooo!

THIS IS CLEARLY A VERY BAD THING.

There has never been a clearer case of messing with forces you don't understand!

WE'VE GOT COMPANY, BAD COMPANY.

Being brave is as easy as being scared, but with less worry.

HE'S CUTE, BUT UNSTABLE – JUST MY TYPE

BRAINWASHING IS NOT ETHICAL.

WHEN SOMEONE TELLS ME I CAN'T DO SOMETHING, I JUST HAVE TO DO IT.

WE'VE GOT TO SAVE MITCHELL, THE SCHOOL, AND GIVEN THE CHANCE - THE WORLD!

I BELIEVE YOU; I BELIEVE ANYTHING.

HIDING IS NOT THE ANSWER!

GREETINGS TO TEMPLETON

Some say Templeton landed on earth during a meteor shower from the planet Baloney. Others reckon he was raised in the wild by disused, artificially intelligent vending machines. He is a **MAGNET** for Temp events, so when an adventure shoots down strange street, Templeton has a knack for making it stranger.

Whatever happens in reality, Mitchell and Becky can always rely on their brainbox friend for a weird alternative Temp theory. He relishes probing, meditating and scheming, but Templeton's suspicions are wrong every time (although bizarrely amusing).
In fact, Templeton is so full of **IMAGINATION** he's not sure where fantasy ends and real life begins.
Templeton is ... templetony. He worships everything, he's a great dancer, makes a really useful household appliance and is not a bad form of transport.
Everyone needs a Templeton!

Becky: Don't worry. There's no such thing as fate.
Templeton: Yes, there is. Or we'd fall over.
Becky: No, Templeton, that's feet. I'm talking fate. You know, Kismet? Destiny?
Templeton: The mean girls in year eight?
Becky: No, the idea that we can't change our future.

WE ARE MOST CERTAINLY ON A SPACECRAFT.

How will I know how it works if I don't take it apart and break it?

SOLVE IT WITH SCIENCE AND SCHEMES.

ROCKET SHOES ENGAGE.

I MUST MEDITATE ON THIS.

INITIATING PANIC PHASE.

ALL DREAMS ARE ILLOGICAL.

MILLIONS OF VIEWERS ARE COUNTING ON ME.

Victory and chewy chocolatey nougat are ours!

CLASHING CLASSMATES

Mitchell, Becky and Templeton's classmates are each strange in their own nutty way. From bullies to geeks, beauties to freaks, all the usual suspects roam the halls, along with oddballs you haven't imagined yet.

STEPHANIE BETHANY

O-M-ME, so shiny!

MATTHEWS

Would you mind terribly if I went berserk?

MIKI & MIKIKO

Glow junk, fun!

GAZZA TAGGIT

Watch your step

SAMIA SPEED

If there's a character that pops wheelies as she sings, I'm it.

You make me proud to be a troublemaker.

LUCAS MONTGOMERY

BISHOP

YOU AIN'T THE KING OF BLING, THAT'S MY THING YO.

TYSON GRIMM

I DON'T JOKE ABOUT NO BOOK! NOT EVEN A JOKE BOOK, FOOL!

CROYDONIA PUTTOCK

I've eaten steaks tougher than you.

15

STRANGE STAFF

MISS GRIMSHAW
I'm the school secretary. No, I don't have a sense of humour or any patience, but I do see and hear everything. I monitor the school's cameras and speakers. My top rules are: no running, no evil cackling, and NO lateness.

MR ABERCROMBIE
I'm the headmaster and what I say goes. I demand the utmost seriousness. I'm not a fool who falls for anything; it has to be good. We respect all students here, no matter how weird they are. But beware, my eyes are on you. EYES ON YOU!

Miss Grimshaw loves it when I get into trouble. One evil lady.

Abercrombie oversees the disasters at SHH, but he never sees that they've got nothing to do with me!

The Librarian is plain freaky.

THE LIBRARIAN
Don't come to my library. You and your awful sticky fingers are not welcome! If you must enter, talk quietly and don't read the books – you'll get paper cuts. Going is good. Goodbye.

NIMROD
I'm an amazing maths machine made in 1959, when children paid respect and attention to teachers. You should know that I've been programmed to humiliate. Confused does not compute – I know the answer to every question and expect you to know too.

Nimrod's an old bucket of bolts that needs updating, fast. For me, to be logical is illogical.

In the entire history of the world, there has never been such an annoying crew of irregular staff in one school. For Mitchell, they're either causing trouble or not helping with trouble. Completely cuckoo! Here are the thoughts of just a few, plus Mitchell's view too.

COOK

It's best not to know what goes on in the kitchen. Just eat your cold hot-dog goulash and chocolate swirly log. If you don't like sugar, you're going on my strange list. Complaints about smells are not allowed.

MURDOCH

Arrr! Most of my time is taken up fixing this shoddy shell of a school. Otherwise I'm on the roof with a harpoon made out of a plunger. Good luck in whatever the heck it is you're doing. And be careful with your limbs – I warn ye!

Murdoch growls a lot and doles out ominous warnings....

Cook's school dinners rule. Sugar for main course and dessert = wicked!

MR BALDING

History is nothing unless it's lived in. So don't rush through it, kids. The key to understanding life is taking it slowly. I know an awful lot and I feel like I've been here forever. Now, have I told you about the interesting history of bread?

MR KANDINSKY

Art is nothing but fun, driven by extreme suffering. I only want emotion. Throw your inner demons in the air, catch them with a brush and smear them crazily on your canvas. Now capture that terror!

Mr Kandinsky tries to get art out of me, but he only gets mess.

Mr Balding blabs painfully slowly. I know he means no harm, but he's a drone in my ears!

STRANGE STAFF CONTINUED...

MR DOUGHERTY

Aroo! I'd like you to make an appointment to see me, as I'm very busy marking on the 4th floor. It's probably better if you don't surprise me as I've been known to bite and my bite is worse than my bark. Don't let my clothes deceive you – I'm definitely a were-teacher.

MR CREEPER

Come on you bunch of layabouts. Action is what you need – step lively! I'm your P.E. teacher, not the librarian! Come on, come on, come on my kookaburras. Remember to breathe.

Say Mr Dougherty's name to see lightning! And watch out for his wolf teeth....

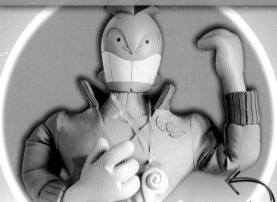

Mr Creeper is a plant grown in the spooky greenhouse that once tried to take over the school. Don't trust a P.E. teacher as far as you can throw them, I say.

MISS GRACKLE

It's true that I like to say and sing my mind. It's probably best not to trust me with any secrets or expect sympathy or encouragement.

Miss Grackle is a highly strung music boff who's as blunt as a mean monkey.

MR GARDENER

Learning is the most fantastic thing you can do and as your English teacher I'm thrilled to share the wonderful world of reading with you. Just do what comes naturally – imagine.

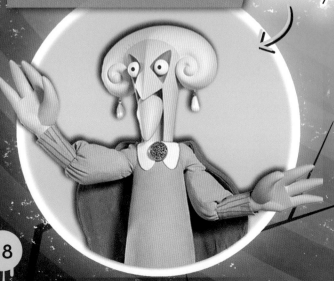

Mr Gardener is the most upbeat teacher. He's so cheery it's eerie.

MYSTERIOUS ME

How would you fit in at Strange Hill High? Fill in your transfer request and prepare your file for an interview with Headmaster Abercrombie. Mitchell, Becky and Templeton will watch out for you!

NAME:.................................

AGE:.................................

BIRTHDAY:.................................

BEST MATE:.................................

CURRENT SCHOOL:.................................

TRANSFER REQUEST TO: Strange Hill High

FAVOURITE HOBBY:.................................

FAVOURITE SCHOOL SUBJECT:.................................

TOP TALENT:.................................

BIGGEST FEAR:.................................

IF YOU WERE A HEAD TEACHER, WHAT WOULD YOU CHANGE ABOUT SCHOOL? ....
....

BEST THING YOU'VE LEARNED AT SCHOOL: ....
....

I THINK YOU KNOW WHAT ALL THIS TUT-TUT-TUTTING AND CLICK-CLOCK-CLUCKING IS ABOUT!

TUT TUT-TUT CLICK-CLOCK

TOILET TURMOIL

It's not everyday a medieval knight comes back to life and does silly things to a bunch of school kids. Sir Bogivere is the Guardian of the Foul Latrine and it was Mitchell who unwittingly woke him. He also awakened He Who Cannot Be Flushed – the slippery, slurping creature that is the accumulation of 1000 years of foulness, plus the occasional peanut. Help Mitchell through the tentacle trap!

START
↓

FINISH
↓

YOU'RE LOOKING A LITTLE... FLUSHED.

GRACKLE SHACKLE

The Grackle from Becky's nightmare held her confidence hostage until she realised she had to do the one thing she was scared of – be the star of the show. Tackle the Grackle puzzle! Fit the missing jigsaw pieces into the correct spots in the picture. Which two pieces don't fit?

YOU CAN RUN FROM YOUR FEARS, BUT YOU CAN'T HIDE. CAN YOU HELP ME FIND BECKY NOT HIDING?

1   2   3   4   5   6   7

ALIEN WORSHIP

As far as Templeton can see, aliens have abducted him.
Which kind, he can't tell. Draw a reflection of awesome aliens
in his glasses. The madder the better!

OH BRILLIANT AND
WONDERFUL SPACE
COWBOYS, I BOW DOWN
TO YOUR SUPERIORITY.
TAKE ME TO
YOUR LEADER.

Which one of you
brought a spaceship
armada to school?

Oi T-town,
worshipping aliens is
weird, even for you.

22

TIME TWISTERS

A clock tower glitch has caused the day to tumble upside down and round and round. Mitchell, Becky and Templeton's story has jumbled into the wrong order! To save them, label the pictures in 1–10 in order of the episode Lost and Found. Write a list of five cool and amazing things you could do with the ability to time travel. Mitchell has already chosen 'All-day lunch'.

All-day lunch

. . . .

. . . .

. . . .

. . . .

. . . .

Soon a long list of stuff is lost.

An old man asks Mitchell if he has seen his son.

Becky, Templeton and Mitchell sneak into the Lost and Found room.

Mitchell's locker is the way out of the Lost and Found.

Abercrombie's desk goes missing!

The friends find the missing things by playing a game of treasure hunt.

Peter Dustpan appears! He wants to play games ... forever....

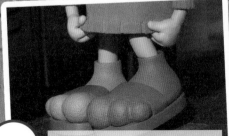
Someone swipes Templeton's trousers!

Peter and his dad are reunited.

Outside, Becky, Mitchell and Templeton show Peter his missing treasure.

TEAM TROUBLE

Tyson, Lucas and Bishop mismatch in many ways, yet this trio of rascals band together to pick on other kids. Can you spot the eight differences between these two pictures?

I CALL IT SURVIVAL OF THE STRANGEST.

GRUESOME GRAFFITI

Gazza Taggit is an awesome graffiti artist. He has the ability to spray paint a picture on any surface, window or wall. It's usually a cool tag of something strange he's seen that day, or a random phrase he's overheard. Then Gazza exits the scene sharpish to watch reactions from afar. Complete this page with a shocking design to knock Abercrombie's socks off.

That tag is da bomb!

25

KING MITCHELL

Mitchell and Becky find Templeton frantically cleaning the boys' toilets. He screams every time he touches the latrines! Their geeky friend is convinced that he's taking part in a cleaning challenge on a reality TV show. Mitchell and Becky exchange looks. It's another abnormal day at Strange Hill High with their imaginative pal Templeton.

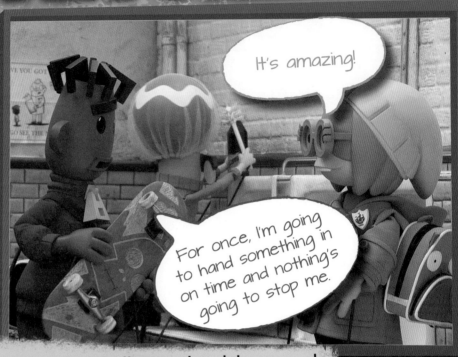

It's amazing!

For once, I'm going to hand something in on time and nothing's going to stop me.

Becky is impressed with Mitchell's woodwork homework. He's carved a design on the bottom of his skateboard.

Mitchell. Becky. So nice to run into you.

UGH!

I'd have preferred to run over you.

As Becky runs along, Mitchell busts some tricks on his skateboard along the hallway until the duo bounce off Tyson's big belly.

Tough guy Tyson wants to swipe Becky's woodwork project, which is a wooden sweater. Instead of handing it over, Mitchell whacks Tyson on the head with the wooden sweater and he and Becky split the scene. Tyson charges after them!

GRRRRRRRR!

A scuffle leads to Tyson rocketing into the boys' toilets on Mitchell's wheels.

The bulky bully crashes headfirst into a wall, cracking it and smashing Mitchell's skateboard!

Tyson is OK, but it looks like Mitchell won't be handing in his homework anytime soon.

Mitchell and Becky pull at some loose plaster on the wall to reveal ancient wooden slats and then... A door! Inside is a secret chamber that looks really old. There's a statue of a knight and an evil-looking toilet that makes demonic glurpy noises. Stranger and stranger... Mitchell finds a nice oak table, which gives him a really sweet idea...

It's a door! I love doors! Even more than walls!

Ah! Toilet of the Gods....

Abercrombie catches Mitchell dragging the table through the toilets and scoffs with disbelief when Mitchell tries to explain.

Suddenly, the table starts to glow and strange singing echoes around the stalls. Abercrombie suspects something rather irregular is going on.

Sir, I swear that I made this table and that I, Mitchell Tanner, am its one true owner.

You want me to believe that YOU made an antique gold inlaid oaken table?

27

The statue of the knight is glowing too and it begins to rumble and wobble.

Becky and Tyson yelp and shake in terror while Templeton watches calmly. The stone shatters to reveal a real knight underneath!

WHOA

Mitchell giggles as he races into the chamber.

You mean I can...
Yes
And you'll do whatever I...
Yes

Outside, Sir Bogivere dances like a cheerleader, waving pom-poms to bad pop music.

Mitchell controls the boom box like a true king. He doesn't want to listen to Becky's advice to tell Sir Bogivere that he isn't really a king – he's having too much fun wondering what other things Sir Bogivere will do.

The knight is called Sir Bogivere, Guardian of the Foul Latrine, and he swears loyalty to King Mitchell, the owner of the Round Table.

Mitchell realises that this means he can ask Sir Bogivere to do anything he asks, so he decides to take the ancient bodyguard for a test drive...

I know only that I would lay down my life to protect you.

Cool. Can you do algebra?

28

During a maths exam, Sir Bogivere defends Mitchell against Nimrod's wicked wizardry (aka algebra).

Bogivere brings down his sword on Nimrod's cord, causing sparks to fly! For Sir Bogivere, the electric snake that held its spell over the vile box has been slain; for Nimrod it's time for a sleep.

Tyson, Lucas and Bishop try to corner Mitchell before running away from Sir Bogivere into the secret chamber and locking the door.

You dare assault my liege with your diabolical incantations!

YAY!

AAGGHH!

Listen up, you caused my mate here considerable embarrassment what with his foolish head-smack into the toilet wall. The second your Sir Fruitypants ain't around, you're gonna get it.

Sir Bogivere explains that the bullies are now trapped with the latrine that is connected to the Pit of Eternal Damnation – loathsome things could happen! Mitchell isn't fussed, but he doesn't realise that tentacles of foul black ooze have already bubbled out of the ancient toilet....

As Becky and Templeton fan him with large leaves, Mitchell reclines on a bench, potato crisp crumbs on his face.

He's too lazy to reach for his drink and asks his knight to do it for him before ironing his socks.

My royal feet feel most untoasty.

It troubles me sire, that these quests lack a certain gravitas.

29

Abercrombie tells Mitchell off for issuing orders like a king around school and marches him to the toilets for clean-up duty.

To stop Sir Bogivere from stopping the headmaster, Becky has to reveal that Mitchell isn't really a king. The knight realises he's been duped!

He just kind of lied....

Betrayed by a boy of twelve!

UH-OH.

Stand and face me, false king.

Mitchell and Templeton enter the toilet, bog brushes in hands. Mitchell calls to Sir Bogivere to clean the toilets for him, but the knight leaps out from inside a stall, brandishing his sword.

The only way to regain his besmirched honour is a battle with Mitchell! And Sir Bogivere's got Becky prisoner in a stinky cage, so Mitchell can't wiggle out of it!

Mitchell explains that these days, you don't fight with swords. A round of Rock, Paper, Scissors will do the trick.

Templeton steps up to umpire the duel and after the count of three, Sir Bogivere and Mitchell begin.

TA-DA!

Draw!

They draw again. The tension is high as the pair draw once more. Another point to Mitchell!

Only a madman would draw scissors three times.

30

It's no use, it's stuck on!

With a crash the ancient doors unlock and Lucas falls out, yelling. A giant tentacle slithers past and grabs him back. He Who Cannot Be Flushed has awoken! Lots more tentacles lash about and Mitchell and Sir Bogivere battle to defeat the gunky creature.

While Sir Bogivere is carried away, a tentacle snakes around Mitchell's leg as he desperately reaches for the toilet cleaner. The label reads 'Excalibur! Legendary cleaning power!'

But Mitchell frees the bottle! Mitchell bravely fights his way into the ancient chamber, waving the cleaner. Shafts of magical liquid cut through the tentacles like a lightsaber.

Becky and the boys are freed, and then Mitchell manages to save Sir Bogivere from a long drop down the Well of Despair.

AAGGHH!

Becky and Mitchell survey the damage in the boys' toilets. It's total carnage and Abercrombie is due to inspect Mitchell's cleaning work any second. What are they going to do? He's coming in!

Let's clean up!

Mitchell holds the mighty Excalibur cleaning bottle aloft, hoping for a miracle. Rays of light shine in every direction and Becky holds her breath, waiting for the inevitable clamour from Abercrombie.

Ooo!

ZING!

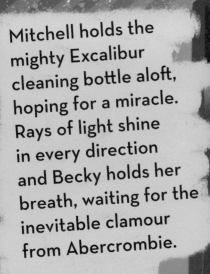

Well I suppose it will have to do.

The headmaster stops short, stunned by the sight that greets him. Abercrombie has never seen such a sparklingly clean lavatory.

It is incredible, but he shuffles out with a grudging grunt.

Mitchell, Becky and Templeton help Sir Bogivere push the Round Table back into the secret chamber. He is to return to his duty as Guardian of the Foul Latrine.

I must guard against the evil effluent should the sewers of darkness threaten the world once more.

The friends have saved the world, but there's still one problem. With the Round Table sealed away, what is Mitchell going to hand in for his woodwork project?

How quickly can you knit a wooden suit of armour?

WOODWORK WONDER

Save Mitchell from detention by creating a new woodwork design on his second skateboard. Phew!

THE DAILY WEEKLY

JUNIOR JUMBLE

Abercrombie is often defeated by the Junior Jumble crossword in the school paper.
Help the stuffy head teacher complete this word puzzle before he storms into a sulk!

BLAST AND BOTHER! THIS CROSSWORD IS AS TOUGH AS COOK'S SPAGHETTI.

ACROSS

3. Another word for idiot. (11)
   A................

5. The reason why Mitchell becomes a reporter. (2, 7) (2 words)

7. Guest photographer for the special edition. (9) T................

8. Mitchell's funniest typo – instead of 'wigs' he wrote 'p.......'. (4)

9. The strange ink that Mitchell uses to print his special edition of the newspaper. (8)

DOWN

1. Name of the school paper. (5, 6)
   The D.......... W.......... (2 words)

2. The editor of the newspaper (9) C ....

4. Instead of lies, reporter Mitchell writes this. (5, 4) T.......... P.........
   (2 words)

6. Mitchell and Becky's hairy surprise. (5) B...........

7. How Mitchell spreads the real news. (2) T....

RADICAL READ

The library is a mysterious place where few students dare to tread. Tucked in a stack of sinister books is a terminal title – a book so boring it has opened a borehole in space and time. The only way out is to read a thrilling adventure. Add your own amazing chapter to the story of Strange Hill High!

Watch out for the book bugs.

No beat-boxing and no paparazzi in the library.

This goes against my every instinct, but I've got to read that book.

SPOOKY EYES

EYES ON YOU

Abercrombie can't wait to catch out Mitchell. He is convinced he's a troublemaker! And Mitchell is sure Abercrombie's glaring look is everywhere. How many gunky eyeballs can you count?

.... EYEBALLS

SHADOW SEARCH

Bocky is a friendly pal made from weird, unnaturally reanimated mud. She first began as Templeton's clay statue of Becky, but a spark of electricity brought her to life.
Which shadow shape belongs to Bocky?

SCHOOL IS EVEN FREAKIER AFTER DARK. YOU WON'T CATCH ME IN THERE!

TAMPERED EVIDENCE

Templeton's photographic evidence has been tampered with! He sang into a banana so the culprit could be the Lord of the Apes! Re-order each photo to spell a word.

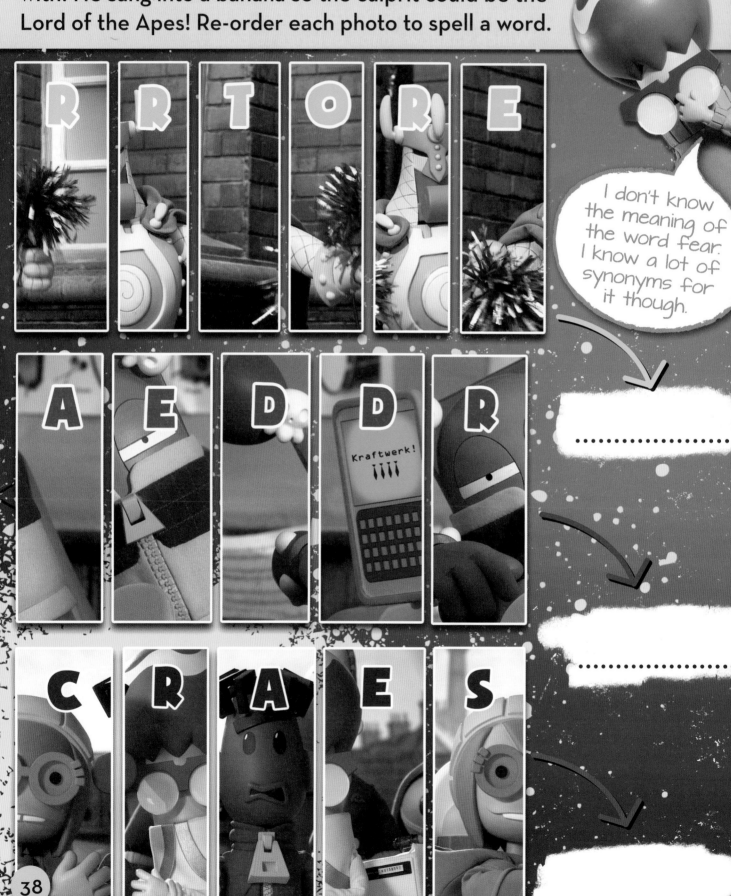

I don't know the meaning of the word fear. I know a lot of synonyms for it though.

FUNKY FUZZ

Something bizarre is going on! Mitchell and Becky are turning invisible! Bring the duo back to reality by joining the dots in the correct order. Then draw beards on both friends. Why? WHY NOT?

39

THE END OF TERMINATOR

Something strange is going on at Strange Hill High. The school is looking shoddier than usual. Everything seems to be old or broken.

AHH!

The machines in this school aren't evil; they're just hopelessly out of date.

Mr Garden tries to photocopy a page from the book Dante's Inferno and the photocopier catches fire!

Stephanie taps a few keys and her computer sparks and shatters.

BANG!

Umm...

Within a few minutes, Mr Balding's pencil sharpener ignites and the clock in the classroom explodes.

ecky thinks Nimrod, the ancient omputerised maths instructor, must e malfunctioning too because she ets a 'C' in her maths exam. Mitchell is annoyed that he's failed he test so he decides to get his own pack on the bucket-of-bolts teacher. Nimrod's programmed to answer any question, but what if it's a trick question? Mitchell asks Nimrod a simple but impossible question to answer.

WHIR

2 plus 2 equals 5. Is the answer yes or no?

Brilliant! If he answers "yes", then he hasn't answered the question correctly because the answer is "no", but he can't say "no" because that means the answer is not "no".

You are attempting to confuse me. I cannot be confused. I am the amazing Nimrod. You are Tanner. You know nothing.

The kids call out different contrary things. Nimrod shakes in confusion and threatens to fail them all. This last thought causes sparks to fly – Nimrod short-circuits and his lights go out.

N.I.M.R.O Compe

UH-OH

That's the one thing I do know. That I know nothing at all. Compute that!

The next day, Mitchell is looking forward to spending maths class looking out the window, when a shiny new teacher-bot catches him by surprise. She sure is different. Cate is a Computerised Automated Teaching and Educational unit. The first thing Cate suggests is spending class outside in case they find an ice-cream truck. Could Cate be the best ever teacher?

I'm programmed to be nurturing and understanding. And to make learning fun!

41

Abercrombie announces that Strange Hill has undergone a complete mechanical upgrade. All things old have been brought up to date and they have an exciting new language lab.

BLAH, BLAH...

The whole lot is linked to the master system, including the CCTV. The headmaster knowingly warns Mitchell that his attempts to test the system will come to no good, but Mitchell simply blows raspberries at the camera.

Cate continues to charm the students in her classroom who sigh and giggle with happiness. She is really soothing and sweet. Templeton can't help having a crush on the perfect computerised lady. Becky is wooed by her new role model too.

Whuzzat, now?

Luv in the digital era, yo!

Mitchell's banter brings him to Cate's attention and she asks him to answer the maths problem on the board. Mitchell squirms, so Cate kindly moves on. Mitchell stares in disbelief. This teacher is super nice!

I'll call on another student until you're ready. Take your time.

42

Unknown to the kids, Cate's internal view is different to what she says. Her inner scanner reveals that Mitchell is identified as a potential troublemaker.

The words 'neutralise all threats' blink across her screen.... Phase one is being initiated.

Soon it becomes clear that Cate is the voice for all the new kit around the school, including the new milk dispenser in the canteen. Templeton is delighted, though Mitchell thinks it's a little creepy.

Oh, pardon me, chums. I didn't mean to block your way. I'd be happy to step to the side.

Cate seems to be everywhere!

Mitchell and Becky bump into a weird-looking Tyson shape. His eyes are a bit glassy and his voice is more polite than usual.

The friends are freaked by his abnormal reaction and quickly zip past.

EUGH?

43

Mitchell is sure something fishy is going on, so he and Becky visit their new teacher to ask her if she is part of a vast electronic conspiracy to turn the students into a bunch of goody-goody zombies. Also, has she ever associated with any known werewolves?

Cate chuckles and brushes the questions away as nonsense. As soon as Mitchell and Becky leave, she turns to a glowing red screen.

They're asking too many questions. Initiate master protocol.

Mitchell and Becky hide behind the classroom door and peer through the window to see Cate developing her evil plan.

They figure out that Cate is using the new language lab to control the school and soon the world. Mind control in every language on earth – impressive and scary at the same time!

HMM

She's like the Terminator! The end-of-terminator!

Mitchell knows that they need an equally sophisticated computer system, one that can go head to head with one of the most advanced, diabolical electronic minds ever created....

They plug in Nimrod instead and reveal the trouble in town.

Nimrod is sure he can help and tells Mitchell, Becky and Templeton how he was built to play war games in the Cold War.

WOW!

Wow! He's the perfect weapon!

44

The zombification of the school has got much worse. Cate is in complete control and it looks like she has an army of zombies!

The zombies have unnaturally bright eyes and are all very polite.

It's time to strike at the heart of the matter, or Mitchell, Becky and Templeton will get sucked into the new bizarre order too.

Nimrod advises that an army runs on its stomach, so the team choose to confront them in the dining hall with an army of their own – an army of Nimrod-aged machines! They march, roll and wobble to battle.

Lovely day in the hallway, inn't?

To the dining hall and on to victory!

And hopefully lunch! Fighting evil makes me hungry.

Mitchell throws open the doors to the dining hall and gasps at the strange sight of calmness and regularity. It's very eerie.

Where's the happy talking? Where's the fun? Where's the person pouring creamed spinach on Templeton's head? Even Abercrombie is a pleasant automaton.

We're all in our places with bright shiny faces.

45

In her most noble voice, Becky calls on her fellow pupils to liberate themselves from perfect behaviour and Nimrod's army storms (as quickly as possible) into the room.

Mitchell starts a food fight and the serious scene goes crazy! Machines and dinner become a messy mix as goo is flung around.

WAHOO!

Hysterical laughter fills the hall and Mitchell rides around on Nimrod, reveling in the glory of chaos.

Templeton knows things are getting back to normal when he's covered with creamed spinach.

Now we're talking!

Cate arrives to halt the mayhem, but she's too late. Mitchell will do anything to avoid learning. He calls for Nimrod's ramming speed and the pair zoom to Cate and the 'bots battle.

At last Cate is buried under the spoils from an old vending machine. The devious mind-control experiment is over and the school is back to being a shoddy mess.

Victory and chewy chocolatey nougat are ours!

Next time I'll save the world neatly.

END OF TERM QUIZ

HOW CLOSELY DID YOU STUDY THE STORY? TEST YOUR KNOWLEDGE WITH THIS TRICKY QUIZ.

1. Which maths grade was Becky disappointed with?

☐ a) C
☐ b) D
☐ c) B

2. Nimrod described himself as....

☐ a) Ace
☐ b) Awesome
☐ c) Amazing

3. Which kind of question did Mitchell ask Nimrod?

☐ a) Crazy
☐ b) Clever
☐ c) Impossible

5. Cate won the class over with which food?

☐ a) Ice cream
☐ b) Ice lollies
☐ c) Icicles

4. What does CATE stand for?

☐ a) Computerised Automated Technology and Educational unit
☐ b) Computerised Automated Teaching and Educational unit
☐ c) Computerised Advanced Teaching and Educational unit

6. Name the new type of room SHH opened with the tech upgrade.

☐ a) Singing studio
☐ b) Language lab
☐ c) Computer lab

7. What colour screen did evil Cate have?

☐ a) Blue
☐ b) Green
☐ c) Red

8. The zombies were extremely....

☐ a) Rude
☐ b) Polite
☐ c) Polished

9. Experience with which games made Nimrod a perfect weapon?

☐ a) War games
☐ b) Computer games
☐ c) Word games

CRAZY CALENDAR

Monday	Tuesday	Wednesday	Thursday
1. Write a MC Bonebag rap about something big that happened in your day.	2. Choose a Strange Hill student and stay in character from breakfast until dinner.	3. Walk backwards to where you want to go.	4. Bake a chocolate swirly log.
8. Practise your SHH evil cackle.	9. Learn a new yo-yo trick.	10. Try to have a rhyming conversation with a friend.	11. Make a weird cartoon character of yourself.
15. Practise a secret handshake.	16. Make a plan in case giant pets invade.	17. Keep a ghost diary.	18. Talk in slow motion, then really fast.
22. Make a costume and props for an adventure with Templeton.	23. Pretend you are on a reality TV show.	24. Experiment with different coloured water to make new potions.	25. Answer every question with a question.
29. Make a strange song playlist for a school trip.	30. Design a new wrapper for SHH's Chocolate Insanity Bar.	31. Write funny captions for school photos.	

48

If your life isn't strange enough, try something new every day – either with your family, friends or by yourself. Be inspired by this unusual timetable and have a go at making your own.

Friday	Saturday	Sunday
5. Sing a story as if your life was a musical.	6. Think up a monstrous menu for lunch.	7. Make a self-portrait with words instead of a picture.
12. Find a new hiding place at school.	13. Change the numbers on your clock to food pictures. Pizza o'clock?	14. Read a book with a boring cover.
19. Hide a time capsule about your life for time travelers to find.	20. Write a news story for The Daily Weekly.	21. Create a wacky poster for the SHH notice board.
26. Think of five surprises to spring on your friends.	27. Talk in a strange accent.	28. Remember five random excuses for being late.

BALDING BUSTER

A most unfortunate side effect of Mr Balding's class is mind-bending boredom. This strange word puzzle is the perfect antidote to a dull lesson. Avert fossilisation by finding all the words that end in 'y'.
Look up, down, forwards, backwards and diagonally.

```
F R E A K Y Y G Y Q B Y V C M
X Y K K X B G K I C U X O U P
Y R A S L T A K E J H I X C L
P A V C B E D O O E D T R A C
E C D F N Q H O P X G X V K G
E S O S C L C K C F U X C F Y
R C O R O S K Y M Q C N S N B
C B A Z H I R W L M Q I O W K
I Z C F Y W S P O O K Y A B W
Y O I L W K F Q J S Y K A E P
F K L D O W A C K Y H K L U J
C I Z W K P Y V M Q E N K A V
S C B A C Q O N E E D O N S W
K L B X H U D T B A C C N L P
J K T D L I U V I J N G L A I
```

WHY-OH-WHY? MUST KEEP EYES OPEN.

- ☐ CREEPY
- ☐ SNEAKY
- ☐ FREAKY
- ☐ KOOKY
- ☐ QUIRKY
- ☐ CRAZY
- ☐ PEAKY
- ☐ GEEKY
- ☐ SCARY
- ☐ SILLY
- ☐ WACKY
- ☐ SPOOKY

School time is not time for thinking.

50

DETENTION DOODLES

Mitchell often gets through detention by doodling spaceships on his homework. This time he's inspired by the Mr Creeper creature – a plant that, when energised up by extreme fertiliser, took over the school to make it a monster CO2 producing factory as rare as rocking horse poo. Complete this page from Mitchell's 'work' book with awesome art depicting the invasion of the vines. Make Mr Kandinsky proud!

Something creepy, something unknown, something that actually wants to go to school.

This is not what I wanted for my widdle Planty woo.

A VERY SERIOUS EXAM

They take exams very seriously at Strange Hill High, more seriously than anything – even students getting attacked by the wolves on the school moors. This is all ever so serious. The answer to each question is true or false. How many can you get right?

Don't Mitchell this up.

THIS IS TWISTING MY MELON, MAN.

T F

☐ ☐ 1. Becky loves doors even more than walls.

☐ ☐ 2. Abercrombie knows Templeton as 'weird boy'.

☐ ☐ 3. Templeton always looks forward to toilet duty.

☐ ☐ 4. Mitchell was cursed to be a school teacher.

☐ ☐ 5. There is a secret 5th storey of the school.

☐ ☐ 6. Room 101 is otherwise known as The Room of Doom.

☐ ☐ 7. Miss Cate is the best teacher of all time.

☐ ☐ 8. Becky won the secondary school staring seriously semi-finals.

☐ ☐ 9. Templeton speaks sense 50% of the time.

☐ ☐ 10. Samia can speak French.

☐ ☐ 11. Mitchell's locker is a doorway to the Lost and Found room.

☐ ☐ 12. The sweetest tooth in school belongs to Tyson.

☐ ☐ 13. Templeton's gangster name is T-time.

FUME FURY

Templeton is busy with science and schemes. This experiment is entering the danger zone! Which potion will stop the commotion before Templeton initiates panic phase?

THE CURSE OF THE WERE-TEACHER

It's Careers Day and all the kids have been given a job prediction for when they grow up. Mitchell has breakdancing fighter pilot in mind, so he can't believe the result that predicts he will become a teacher! That's the worst job in the world!

Mitchell motors to the staff room to sort out the horrible mistake. The bustling room goes silent when the teachers see a student has entered their inner sanctum of tea and cake.

Tanner! Pupils may not enter the staff room!

AH-HM

We dare not speak his name.

The person you are looking for is the deputy head – Brian Dougherty!

The teachers try not to reveal who the person is that looks after career testing, but instead they say too much about him. Miss Grackle spills the biggest bean! Thunder and lightning follow Brian Dougherty's name, making everyone gasp.

Some people say he went mad from all the paperwork.

Apparently the dangerous Dougherty has been hidden somewhere in the school so he can't harm anyone, but he still processes all the school's paperwork.

Mitchell, Becky and Templeton decide to hunt down the mystery teacher. Matthews says the terrifying fourth floor is a good place to start, before running away in hysterics.

EEK!

The fourth floor is cloaked from normal sight. Some say it only appears in a full moon. At the top of the staircase, they find a cute tiny door inside a normal door, which leads to the creepy higher level....

Aaaggghhh! I've been bitten by a rabid teacher!

As they walk around the cobwebby, shadowy secret storey, Becky notices that everything has been graded in drippy red paint, from the clock to the water fountain. Very weird....

At the far end of the corridor, inside a boarded up office, Mitchell and Becky hear chains rattling. Mitchell ventures in and calls out for Mr Dougherty. Lightning flashes! From the depths of the office wreck, the chains rattle and rattle. A hairy, fanged man looms out of the gloom. Suddenly, he lunges, growls and bites at Mitchell! Mitchell runs to third-floor safety, feeling very strange.

55

The next thing Mitchell remembers is standing in the hallway with a mug of coffee in his hand. Becky is relieved to see her friend when he joins his classmates. She went to get help but ran into an awful new substitute teacher who yelled at her to go straight into class.

Then, thank goodness, he left. Becky doesn't know what's worse. Mitchell's destiny to become a teacher or the new substitute teacher. All the kids have annoying stories about the new substitute teacher. He gave Samia five hours of homework in P.E. and replaced Gazza's spray paint with an air freshener.

He made me sit in the corner and wear this hat.

The Pe...sian War

GRRR

Nobody wants gra-frutti, yo!

Becky remembers that the teacher's name is Tanner and guesses Mitchell might know him, but Mitchell is miffed at the thought. The school bell rings. Mitchell's hand starts to throb so he rushes to the toilet before the next lesson begins.

If I ever see him, I'll let him know who's who!

Within seconds Mitchell begins to change. He loses his style and gains several feet in height, while his hair shrinks and his belly and chin expand. Spectacles pop onto his nose to frame his glare. Mitchell's s transformed into Mr Tanner the teacher! The baddest teacher in all the land. Back in the classroom, Mr Tanner gives a Greek history lesson with as much gruff as he can muster. There will be no giggling in his class, but there will be a surprise quiz.

Abercrombie congratulates Mr Tanner on a job well done. Everything is ship-shape since he came to Strange Hill. Mr Tanner is just pleased to see the children so fearful. Their chat is interrupted by the school bell. Abercrombie is shocked to see Mitchell where his new best friend was only moments before.

Mitchell is pained that he can't get to the one teacher that is causing everyone so much agony.

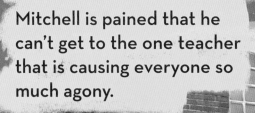

It's like he runs off whenever I come.

Oo, maybe he's scared of you?

Unlikely, he's a very scary guy.

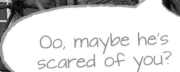

The school bell rings, signalling the end of break. Mitchell begins to change and this time it's in front of his friends.

Help! Whatever this is it's happening again!

Mr Tanner is caught in the jungle gym, causing him to growl fiercely.

Mitchell is Mr Tanner! Mr Tanner is Mitchell! Tanner, Mitchell! Mitchell, Tanner!

EYOW!

The school bell rings again and Mitchell reappears. Mr Dougherty's bite has made Mitchell a were-teacher – and instrument of torment! Could it be more awful?

Mitchell, Becky and Templeton return to the fourth floor to confront Mr Dougherty and save Mitchell.

Becky shines her torch at a chomping noise in the corner. Case in point. Mr D is licking and gnawing feverishly at a bone.

I'm a big jerk and I've got to stop me before my reign of terror goes too far.

Mitchell demands a cure to his mutation problem. According to legend, as long as the infected substitute teacher does not sign a permanent contract with the school, the curse will wear off. Mitchell is really worried that Abercrombie will offer Mr Tanner a full-time job. There must be a way to stop himself being doomed forever!

I'll tell you how, if you release me.

As soon as his chains are broken, Mr Dougherty pounces off the desk and scampers away with a wolfish howl. The kids will have to solve this on their own (as usual). Mitchell has a plan!

58

Abercrombie gushingly welcomes Mr Tanner to the special contract-signing ceremony. He is so excited to have a full-time friend. Unmoved, Mr Tanner is his usual grumpy self.

Let's just sign this thing and get it over with. I gotta lotta kids to yell at before they go home.

But the signing of a teacher's contract is a sacred tradition at Strange Hill. Plus I have dipped strawberries!

Another treat for Mr Tanner is a song of appreciation from Miss Grackle and Miss Grimshaw. Abercrombie puffs with pride – he wrote the song himself and can't help joining in the serenade.

How do you thank someone who gives detention all afternoon?

MR TANNER SIGHS...

Becky listens at the door, holding a walkie-talkie. At just the right moment she signals to Templeton to ring the school bell, which he does with a big mallet.

Stand by for Tanner Time!

Ready for Hammer Time with the Tanner Time!

59

SIGN IT, SIGN IT, SIGN IT, SIGN IT...

Wiggity, wiggity, beepity bool, I'm not signing anything, you creepity fool!

Mr Tanner's head morphs into Mitchell's.

Becky and Templeton use the bell to make Mitchell and Mr Tanner continually switch, causing lots of confusion. Abercrombie doesn't like the Mitchelly behaviour one bit and pleads for Mr Tanner to be normal.

Oops! Templeton falls off his ladder and misses the bell signal! Mr Tanner is left in control and gets ready to sign the dreaded contract. Becky panics – she needs Templeton to ring the bell now!

Templeton leaps up to ring the bell, over and over again, letting Mitchell break free from Mr Tanner. Abercrombie orders Mitchell out of his office immediately.

They did it! Mitchell, Becky and Templeton broke the curse! Plus they might've driven Abercrombie nuts, to boot. What better way to celebrate than wit chocolate-dipped strawberries?

COSTUME GRADES

Mr Dougherty is a grade-making animal. Help the frizzy and frazzled were-teacher grade these costumes with an A, B, C or D. Templeton is clearly the best at props and costumes!

SUGAR CORRUPTION

The evil Tooth Fairy once impersonated the Cook so he could serve sugary treats and steal everyone's teeth to make a Smilaphone instrument. Now the squeaky pixie is at it again! Becky is stuck in a chocolate log loop and can't see straight. Which picture shows the true Tooth Fairy?

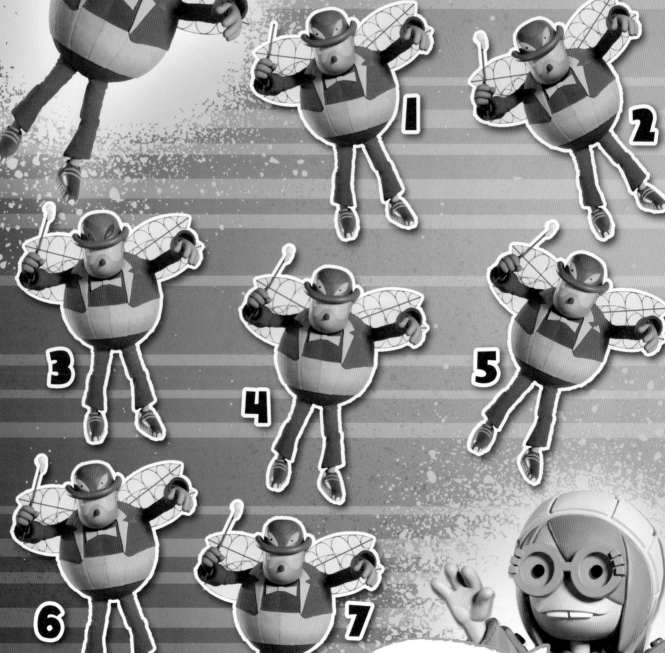

What part of evil fairy inside an automated chef don't you understand?

SCARY ELECTION

Stephanie and Croydonia have collected photos of some of the weirdest events at Strange Hill High and the entire school is electing the top ten. How would you vote? Give each picture a number from 1–10, going up the scary scale so that 10 is the scariest.

SOS VEST

Mitchell quickly learned the ropes at Strange Hill High and made an SOS vest. As far as Mitchell is concerned, it's the only thing that should be considered to be school uniform. Design your own school SOS vest here. You never know when you might need it....

BLOW THE TEACHERS' OLD DUSTY MINDS WITH SOMETHING THAT'S TOO COOL FOR SCHOOL.

SHH

COOL CODES

Becky has a sensible theory. The next time she, Mitchell and Templeton are taken hostage by monsters, weirdos or teachers (or all of the above), they should communicate in code. That way, the confused captors won't be able to figure out the escape plan in time to stop them from fleeing!

PIG LATIN

Take the first consonant of a word, move it to the end of the word and add 'ay'. So, the word 'pig' becomes 'igpay' and the word 'run' becomes 'unray'.

ANIMAL CHATTER

Use an animal sound to substitute a common action. 'Run' could be a startled hedgehog, a burping goat or a coughing giraffe.

DANCE DIVERSION

Pick a dance move for key ideas. You could hop and twirl when you mean to say 'hide'.

Anyone fancy a game of hide and shriek?

I haven't had time to work out my last words. Oh, what if that was them?!

Er. Becks? I don't think you've thought this through.

GAME OF GROANS

At Strange Hill High it can sometimes feel like you're going round in circles. Either that or going round the bend! Will you survive this groan-inducing game? You have to be in it to win it! Eyes on the prize!

1. Play this game with your best friend.
2. Choose to be Mitchell, Becky or Templeton and find something small and random to be your counter, like a badge or a button, and place it on the start.
3. Choose the colour red, blue or green.
4. Take turns rolling the dice and move that number of spaces on the path.
5. Every time you stop on your colour, score a point.
6. You are doomed to keep going round the game until a player scores 15 points – that player is the winner.
7. The winner gets respect. That is all.

4

3

2
Stunned by a boring book. Miss a turn.

1 START

5
Do a little dance along the disco hall. Go forward 2 spaces.

6
Ouch! You've fallen through a trap door. Go back 2 spaces.

20
You're held in eerie energy. Roll a 6 to continue.

19
Hide from Abercrombie in your locker. Return to start.

18

7

8
Peter Dustman teaches you to fly! Scream and roll again!

9
Dodge the Tooth Fairy demon. Leap forward 1 space.

10

11
Gunk surprise! Skid forward 2 spaces.

12

13

14
Tentacle trap! Fight for your life! Wait until you roll a six.

15
Take a chocolate log moment. Wait 2 turns.

16

17
rn into a giant unny and hop backwards 1 space.

THE 101% SOLUTION

Mitchell's having maths trouble. He needs to get 101% on his next five assignments to pass the year. Another dollop of trouble adding to the overall dire situation is the subject of the next homework. It's assignment 51 – the world's hardest assignment.

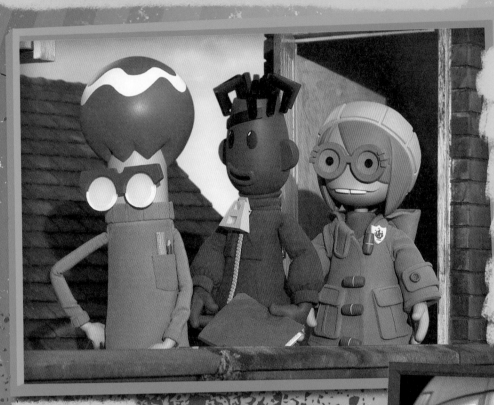

Mitchell acts quickly. He'll cheat! Becky and Templeton help Mitchell swipe the school's file on the legendary Ian Gatlurn. He is the only genius to score top marks on assignment 51. The three friends stealthily assemble on the roof to read their spoils.

Murdoch appears with an ominous warning. Gatlurn solved the unsolvable assignment and terrible things happened. Then the G-Men came and Gatlurn was never seen again.

No one must ever revive the twisted maths Ian Gatlurn conjured in that accursed homework. Before it's too late, I warn ye –

TING!

Mitchell can't risk the possibility of going to summer school (two words that don't belong together). He uses Gatlurn's super complex jottings to answer the assignment and feeds the paper to Nimrod.

At first Nimrod rejects the paper, but Mitchell pushes it back into the computer. Becky is worried that something terrible will happen! Nimrod slowly tots up the score. He starts to shake as the marks stack up for the impossible answers. Mitchell lights up with delight as the score reaches as high as 99%. This could be the best plan he's ever had!

Sparks and smoke overwhelm Nimrod as he shakes under the strain. Mitchell's paper with 101% stamped on it slides out of Nimrod before he bursts into flames. It's game over. Templeton can't understand how Mitchell achieved 101%. It's as impossible as a headmaster with three eyes.

BANG!

On cue, Abercrombie pops up brandishing three eyes. Miki and Mikiko have another identical sister. Templeton has three legs. One plus one appears to be three. Mitchell's broken maths!

Uh-oh

In fact, Mitchell's muddling of the natural order of maths has violated the universe. As he's top of the class the teachers ask him to take some lessons so everyone can learn from his genius mind.

Mitchell happily spreads his made-up-Mitchell maths around the school. Everything he says comes true!

Mitchell's picture replaces Ian Gatlurn's portrait in the hallway soon after he wins four school maths trophies for proving 1=4.

I always hoped that one day it would be ME in a huge undeserved maths genius hallway portrait!

Mitchell, I know praise is wonderful and undeserved acclaim is even more delicious, but DON'T YOU THINK DESTROYING MATHS AS WE KNOW IT MIGHT BE A TAD DANGEROUS?

The school starts to dissolve into maths-based pandemonium. Gazza is looped in infinite repetition!

How could a small hole in the fabric of reality be dangerous?

Matthews floats in the middle of a representation of 10 dimensional spacetime.

AAAGGGHHH!

It tickles!

A sinister G-Man arrives to contain the problem. According to the maths agent, the irregularity will spread until the universe collapses under the weight of its own confusion. The two solutions are: 1) Covering the school with 10,000 tonnes of concrete, 2) Scooping out Mitchell's brain. Time to run from the man with the brain scooper!

YUCK!

The kitchen freezer is a pretty original place to hide. Mitchell and Becky bolt themselves inside and try to think fast.

We've got to do something! I don't like being encased in concrete for eternity! It's not one of my favourite things!

Becky feels someone scratching her head, but it's not Mitchell – it's the extended arm of Ian Gatlurn poking out of his frozen-in-time hotel ice block! They're in luck! Becky and Mitchell set about defrosting Ian. Although they try to be careful, the chipped ice splinters and Gatlurn's head comes off. His eyes flick open, but he speaks more gobbledy-gook than genius....

We need this nerd now!

EW!

The gang plus Gatlurn race along the corridors. Around them, maths is going even more awry. Stephanie pushes the button on the water fountain and equations stream out.

Abercrombie is flattened on the wall like a cartoon.

Tanner! What have you done with my third dimension?!

Mitchell has a great idea. He'll write a new assignment that's so bad it'll get -101%.
That's the way maths will be brought back into balance. As Mitchell sets about his task in Nimrod's classroom, a current of numbers swells across reality.

Gatlurn's gibberish helps Mitchell come up with crazy answers to the questions.

No probloblobob. Norway?

Mitchell hesitates on the last answer. It needs to be a real zinger! Becky yelps at the window. She's trying to keep the concrete-pouring helicopters at bay, but can see the maths phenomenon spreading.

You don't need a wise-crack to save the world, just put anything that's not correct, which is everything in the whole wide world but....

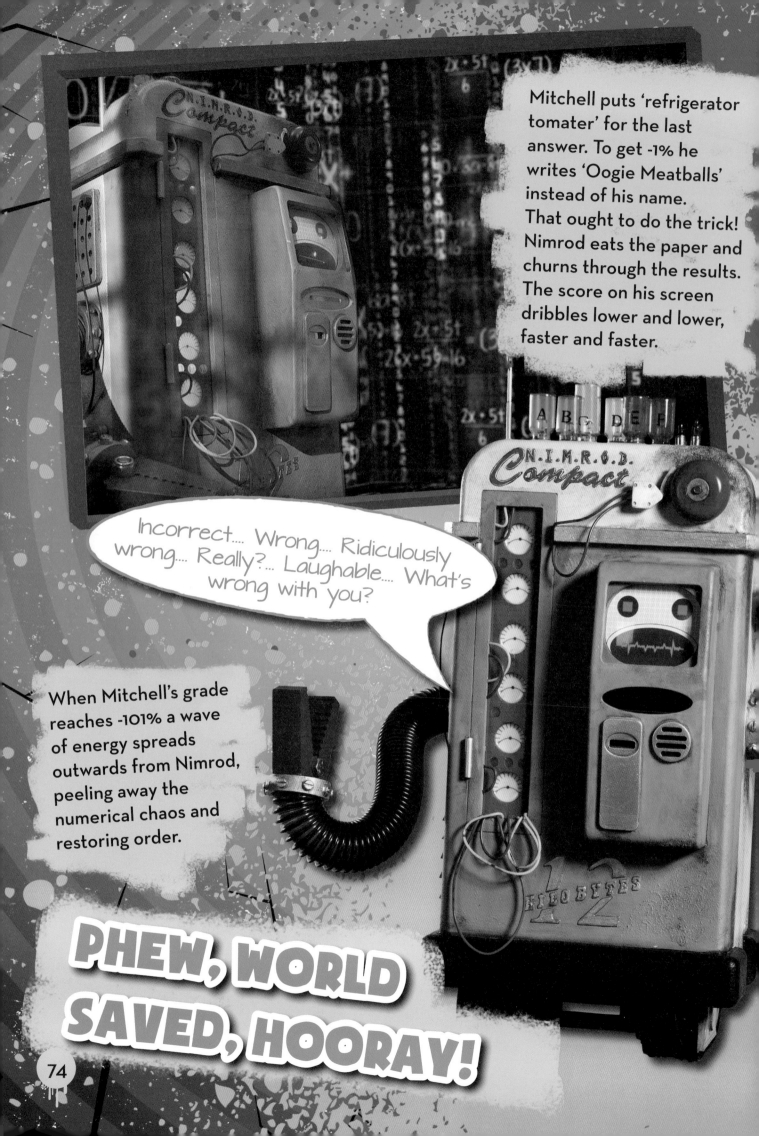

Mitchell puts 'refrigerator tomater' for the last answer. To get -1% he writes 'Oogie Meatballs' instead of his name. That ought to do the trick! Nimrod eats the paper and churns through the results. The score on his screen dribbles lower and lower, faster and faster.

Incorrect.... Wrong.... Ridiculously wrong.... Really?... Laughable.... What's wrong with you?

When Mitchell's grade reaches -101% a wave of energy spreads outwards from Nimrod, peeling away the numerical chaos and restoring order.

PHEW, WORLD SAVED, HOORAY!

WORD = SMART

Wow, with so many number nuggets rolling around, words are needed to balance the brain. Find all the words from the story in this puzzle. Look up, down, forwards, backwards and diagonally.

M	V	T	L	S	J	T	E	P	T	N	C	N	B	R
O	U	X	N	U	B	Q	O	N	L	O	O	A	K	E
U	C	I	E	E	U	R	E	X	A	N	N	U	W	T
I	I	C	A	N	A	C	M	F	O	Q	E	C	M	C	A
J	C	H	T	O	N	R	L	D	T	M	R	V	X	M
C	W	I	A	G	M	P	E	L	E	O	E	V	M	O
Z	O	K	I	O	D	E	B	P	J	N	T	W	K	T
N	D	S	W	H	S	I	D	O	R	E	E	N	U	C
N	S	C	H	E	A	T	M	N	C	H	A	Q	E	H
A	N	R	U	L	T	A	G	E	A	P	A	D	S	Q
S	P	A	C	E	T	I	M	E	N	P	P	U	I	P
D	M	S	Q	O	R	Y	W	T	Y	S	I	U	N	H
X	N	U	K	E	I	U	E	S	H	N	I	G	A	Q
H	F	L	W	N	B	U	M	W	E	T	S	O	Y	Y
K	L	W	Z	A	P	W	I	G	M	Y	P	W	N	X

- GATLURN
- GENIUS
- PANDEMONIUM
- SPACETIME
- CONCRETE
- CHEAT
- EQUATION
- PERCENT
- DIMENSION
- PHENOMENON
- TOMATER
- CHAOS
- ASSIGNMENT

INTRUDER ALERT!

SHH is awash with strange someones and somethings, from the secret cellars to the spooky clock tower. The Transmogrifier has been activated! Imagine the craziest character you can and draw their peaky face around these eerie eyes.

CREEPY AIN'T THE WORD.

THINK OF FIVE UNUSUAL WORDS TO DESCRIBE YOUR STRANGE CREATION.

....

....

....

....

....

ANSWERS

Page 20

Page 21

Page 23

Page 24

Page 34

Page 36

Number of
eyeballs = 61

Page 37

Page 38

1. Terror
2. Dread
3. Scare

Page 47

1. A   6. B
2. C   7. C
3. C   8. B
4. B   9. A
5. A

Page 50

Page 52

1. TRUE   8. TRUE
2. TRUE   9. FALSE
3. FALSE   10. TRUE
4. TRUE   11. TRUE
5. FALSE   12. FALSE
6. TRUE   13. TRUE
7. FALSE

Page 53

Page 62

Number 6

Page 75

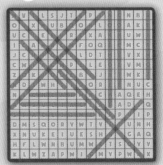

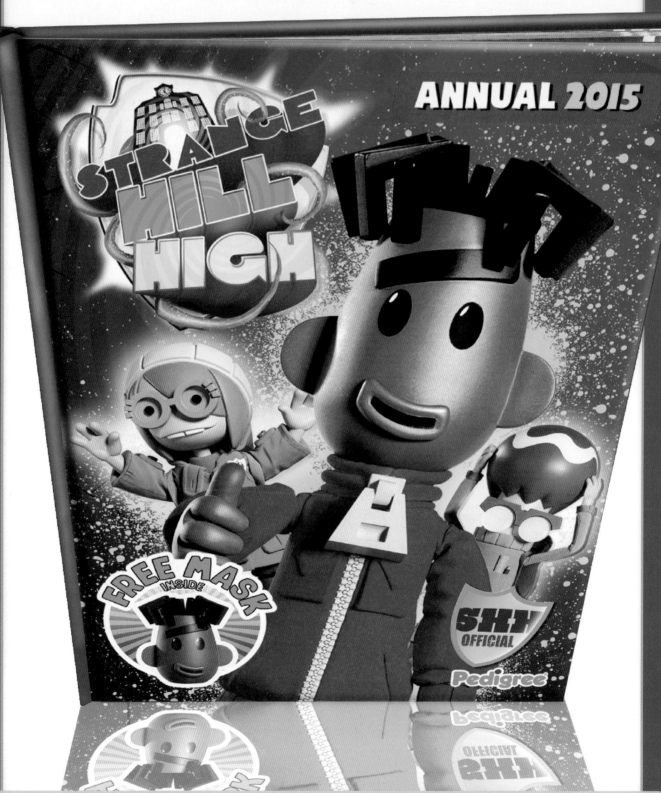